TOGO TO THE RESCUE

How a Heroic Husky Saved the Lives of Children in Alaska

Written by
Mélisande Potter

Illustrated by
Giselle Potter

Christy Ottaviano Books

LITTLE, BROWN AND COMPANY

New York   Boston

In the autumn of 1913, in the town of Nome, Alaska, a Siberian husky named Togo was born. His owner, Leonhard Seppala, a well-known musher, glimpsed the sickly pup with a swollen throat and was sure that Togo would never be the sled-dog racer he'd wished for.

By six months of age, Togo was healthy and very frisky. Whenever Seppala harnessed his work team of six dogs, Togo ran around nipping their ears.

He was so disruptive that Seppala was forced to give him away to a friend. But nothing could stop Togo from running several miles back to Seppala—not even a glass window!

Upon his return, Togo continued to bark and disturb the team, until Seppala finally realized that it was Togo's way of saying "I want to be a team member too!"

Out on the trails
hauling cargo of food
and mail, Togo struggled
to keep in line with the other
dogs, so Seppala released him to
scout for danger ahead. Togo showed no
fear in chasing a feisty reindeer out of the way!

In time, Seppala harnessed Togo to officially join his howling team. Their dog music broke the silence of an unbearably cold, arctic winter that would last for almost eight months.

Togo quickly learned his musher's unique cluck of the tongue before each run. When Seppala saw how keen and adept Togo was, he realized he was the natural-born leader he'd always hoped for and put him at the head of his team.

Daily practice runs over the tundra and curvy landscapes helped the dogs gain prowess, especially with Togo's fighting spirit at the helm.

As Togo matured, Seppala entered his team in sled-racing contests. It was Togo's strength and determination that led them to win many races! After successful runs, Seppala and Togo playfully wrestled in the snow. Their special affection warmed the hearts of those who watched.

In January 1925, when Togo was almost twelve years old, he faced his biggest challenge. There was an outbreak in Nome of a deadly disease called diphtheria. Helpless parents watched in horror while their children suffered from high fevers and struggled to breathe.

If that weren't difficult enough, Nome was stranded in a blasting blizzard.
A serum cure was delivered by train from Anchorage to Nenana, far east of
Nome. But who could collect the serum in the blinding snowstorm? Alaska's
governor, Scott C. Bone, announced that no trains or planes were able to
operate in the severe weather. Families were desperate, until it was agreed
that sled dogs were their only hope.

Seppala packed his sled with dried salmon, seal blubber, blankets, and tools for the six-day emergency journey. Even at his older age, Togo was chosen to lead the team. As they pulled away, all in a weave of padded harnesses, Seppala waved goodbye to his wife and young daughter. He knew all too well that this would be a dangerous trip.

NOME

← TOGO'S TEAM STARTS HERE

GOLOVIN

TOGO'S TEAM HANDS OFF THE SERUM TO THE NEXT TEAM

AND CROSSES THE SOUND

NORTON SOUND

SHAKTOOLIK

TOGO'S TEAM PICKS UP THE SERUM

BERING SEA

ANTITOXIN DIPHTHERIA SERUM

ALASKA

NENANA

← OTHER DOG TEAMS ←
BRING THE SERUM
FROM NENANA TO SHAKTOOLIK

THE SERUM
TRAVELS BY
TRAIN FROM
ANCHORAGE
TO NENANA

In a carefully planned relay race, twenty pounds of the anti-toxin serum were packed in glass vials and passed to different sled teams, which involved 150 dogs as a way to avoid exhaustion. The rescue expedition would cover 674 miles!

ANCHORAGE

To save time, Seppala made the decision to take a treacherous shortcut across Norton Sound by the Bering Sea. He trusted Togo to guide them through wailing winds that blew crystals of ice into their faces. It was nearly impossible to see through the thick sheet of snow, but Togo knew the way and fearlessly charged on.

During the night, the wind increased and blew the ice out to sea.
The ice they were traveling on broke away from the rest.

In a desperate moment, Seppala hurled Togo
five feet to the shore.

When the harness line fell into the sea, Togo instantly reacted with his clever instincts. He grabbed the line with his teeth and rolled around until it was wrapped over his chest to pull Seppala and the team back to shore. Seppala was amazed by Togo's intelligence!

Once on shore, Seppala noticed that Togo was limping and felt a pang of dread. He found a sliver of ice lodged between Togo's toe pads and removed it. To Seppala's great relief, Togo recovered quickly.

After a short rest on beds of birch branches and a filling meal of fish, the team was on its way again.

Night was approaching, and there was no time to lose. Tree branches snapped and owls screeched and zoomed past them as they continued.

Togo carefully navigated the slippery path of a cliff and plowed through tall snowdrifts that could collapse without warning.

He steered his team along jagged ice-capped slopes and led them up and over a five-thousand-foot mountain pass!

After traveling over 250 miles in four and a half days with little rest or food, some of the dogs began to stumble with fatigue.

But Togo persisted, and Seppala pressed them on to Golovin, sixty-five miles east of Nome, where they quickly passed off the serum to the next team of dogs.

Togo and his team had traveled the longest, most difficult part of the race at top speed. As a result, the relay of 150 dogs delivered the crucial medicine to Nome in record time!

The townspeople were overwhelmed with gratitude for their bravery in helping to save the lives of so many children.

One year later, Seppala organized a victory tour across the United States to lecture about Togo's remarkable heroics.

In their final appearance, at Madison Square Garden in
New York City, Togo led his team around the hockey arena
at breakneck speed. The audience burst into applause!

Togo happily panted when he was awarded a gold medal for his bravery. Seppala knew there would never be another dog as loyal, brilliant, and brave as Togo!

AUTHOR'S NOTE

Alaska Natives have always valued dogs as an important part of their families. Dogs haul supplies, help hunt and track, and warn of potential danger.

Alaskan settlers adopted the Native use of dogsleds to transport mail and goods during the long, severe winters. Dogsled drivers, also called mushers, wore the Native fur parkas and boots, or mukluks.

In the early 1900s, there was a gold rush in Nome, Alaska, and thousands of miners flocked to the area. The small, remote town by the Bering Sea was suddenly flooded with immigrants. Among them was a Norwegian man named Leonhard Seppala. Many men and dogs did not survive their first winter, with temperatures sometimes 30 degrees below zero, but Seppala made a name for himself as one of the best mushers working for the Pioneer Mining Company. He quickly became more interested in the dogs than the gold and began competing and winning many sled-dog races. Seppala soon started a kennel for breeding Siberian huskies.

The Siberian husky was brought to Alaska as a stronger, faster sled dog than the mixed breeds that were previously used for work. Siberian huskies have two coats of fur: a coarse overcoat for protection and a thick, softer woolly undercoat for warmth, making them better adapted to the Alaskan climate.

Togo was born at Seppala's kennel in 1913. Even though he was named after the Japanese admiral Tōgō Heihachirō, he was a sickly pup. Seppala's wife, Constance, decided to nurse him back to health. He grew to become Seppala's favorite and most trusted dog and the leader of his team.

In January 1925, a highly contagious disease called diphtheria infected the people of Nome. Mostly affecting children, diphtheria caused high fevers, swollen throats, and blocked airways and was often fatal. To contain the outbreak, children were told to wash their hands with Ivory soap, and the town was put under quarantine. There was a limited supply of anti-toxin serum—liquid medicine that contained antibodies from the blood of recovered patients (or, in this case, horses)—to provide immunity to the sick, and the townspeople were desperate for more to be sent.

That same month, Nome was hit with the worst storm in twenty years, and the only way to transport the serum was by a relay of sled-dog teams. Three hundred thousand glass vials of anti-toxin serum were delivered by train from Anchorage to Nenana, and then needed to get from Nenana to Nome, a distance of 674 miles. The trip was organized into a relay of twenty dog teams with a total of about 150 dogs participating. Seppala had twenty dogs on his team. But for the sake of highlighting Togo, we chose to have a smaller team of nine in the pictures of this book. Each team covered a section of the route, passing off the serum from one team to the next. Seppala's team, led by Togo, traveled the most dangerous part of the relay, crossing the Norton Sound with the shifting ice of the Bering Sea.

In the end, a team led by a young dog named Balto arrived in Nome with the serum. Balto received praise for his role in the rescue even though Togo was the bigger hero. While most teams traveled around thirty miles, Togo's team traveled 261 miles in five straight days. Togo really did leap from the ice and pull his team to shore by tightening the harness line around his body, but it happened on another trip before the serum run. We chose to include this spectacular moment in our telling to further capture Togo's bravery and ingenuity.

The rescue trip is known as the Great Race of Mercy or the Serum Run of 1925. The serum run is still commemorated annually with the Iditarod Trail Sled Dog Race. A year after the run, Seppala brought Togo and his dog team on a tour of the United States, culminating at Madison Square Garden, where Togo was awarded a gold medal.

Togo lived to be sixteen and spent his last years in Maine with a musher named Elizabeth Ricker. She wrote a book called *Togo's Fireside Reflections*. Togo helped autograph several copies with an inked paw. In 2001, a statue of Togo was placed in Seward Park in New York City. In 2011, *Time* magazine named Togo the most heroic animal of all time.

World-renowned Togo

Seppala, Togo (far left), and some of the team on the Nome expedition

SOURCES

The Cruelest Miles: The Heroic Story of Dogs and Men in a Race Against an Epidemic by Gay Salisbury and Laney Salisbury. New York: W. W. Norton, 2003.

Leonhard Seppala: The Siberian Dog and the Golden Age of Sleddog Racing 1908-1941 by Bob Thomas and Pam Thomas. Missoula, MT: Pictorial Histories Publishing Co., 2015.

The Race to Nome: The Story of the Heroic Alaskan Dog Teams That Rushed Diphtheria Serum to Stricken Nome in 1925 by Kenneth A. Ungermann. New York: Harper & Row, 1963.

Togo's Fireside Reflections by Elizabeth M. Ricker. Lewiston, ME: Lewiston Journal Printshop, 1928.

For Pia, Izzy, Adelita, and Felix —MP

For Lottie —GP

About This Book

The illustrations for this book were done in ink and watercolor on watercolor paper. This book was edited by Christy Ottaviano and designed by Tracy Shaw. The production was supervised by Lillian Sun, and the production editor was Jen Graham. The text was set in YWFT Absent Grotesque, and the display type is Woodblock Slab.